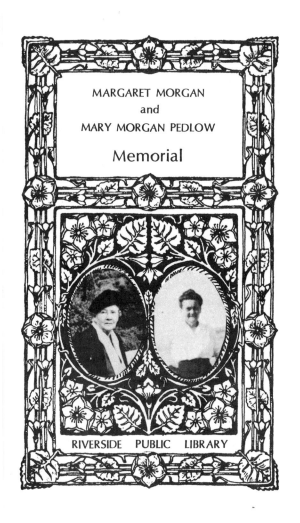

MARGARET MORGAN
and
MARY MORGAN PEDLOW

Memorial

RIVERSIDE PUBLIC LIBRARY

LOG ON TO COMPUTERS

What is a Computer?

Jim Drake

Heinemann Library
Des Plaines, Illinois

© 1999 Reed Educational & Professional Publishing
Published by Heinemann Library,
an imprint of Reed Educational & Professional Publishing
1350 East Touhy Avenue, Suite 240 West
Des Plaines, IL 60018

Designed by Visual Image
Printed in Hong Kong

03 02 01 00 99
10 9 8 7 6 5 4 3 2 1

Library of Congress Cataloging-in-Publication Data

Drake, Jim, 1955-
    What is a computer? / Jim Drake.
        p.   cm. – (Log on to computers)
    Includes bibliographical references and index.
    Summary: A basic introduction to how computers work, describing
bits, and bytes, keyboards, memory, disks, CD_ROMs and software.
    ISBN 1-57572-787-0 (lib. bdg.)
    1. Microcomputers—Juvenile literature. 2. Computer input-output
equipment—Juvenile literature. [1. Microcomputers.
2. Computers.] I. Title. II. Series: Drake, Jim, 1955- Log on
to computers.
 TK7885.5.D73   1999
004-dc21   98-48089
                                                CIP
                                                AC

Acknowledgments
The author and publishers would like to thank the following for permission to reproduce photographs: BBC/O. Upton, p. 29; Trevor Clifford, pp. 4, 5, 10, 11, 12, 13, 14, 15, 16, 18, 20, 21, 23, 24; Format/Sally Lancaster, p. 27; Image Bank/B. Busco, p. 25; K. Mori, p. 22; M. Tcherevkoff, p. 17; Science Photo Library, p. 6; Dr. J. Burgess, p. 8; H. Morgan, p. 26; A. Syred, p. 19; Sygma, p. 7; I. Vimonen, p. 28.
Cover illustration by Andy Parker.

Every effort has been made to contact copyright holders of any material reproduced in this book. Any omissions will be rectified in subsequent printings if notice is given to the Publisher.

Some words are shown in bold, **like this.** You can find out what they mean by looking in the glossary.

CONTENTS

WHAT COMPUTERS DO NOW

Fifty years ago, most people had never heard of computers. This book was written on a computer. Computers helped to put the pictures and words together. The store where the book was bought, and the bank that the money to buy it came from, also use computers.

There are more than 100 million computers like this in the world.

4

Computers can only do what they are told. But they work very quickly. A **program** gives the computer instructions. Programs use special computer languages. They take information from disks, or information that is typed on a keyboard. They change this information into a special code.

Most computers cannot understand human language yet. But they understand the code on this page.

```
jindex.htm

<SCRIPT LANGUAGE = "JavaScript">
function SetCookie (name, value)
{
    var argv = SetCookie.arguments;
    var argc = SetCookie.arguments.length;
    var expires = (argc > 3) ? argv[3] : null;
    var path = (argc > 4) ? argv[4] : null;
    var domain = (argc > 5) ? argv[5] : false;
    var secure = (argc > 5) ? argv[5] : false;
    var val = null;
    if (value != '') val=value;

    if (argc > 2)
        expires = argv[2]

    else
    {
        var expdate = new Date ();
        expdate.setTime (expdate.getTime () + (24 * 60 * 60 *
1000 * 365));    expires = expdate;
    }
    //window.alert(expirest" "+path+" "+domain+" "+secure);
    document.cookie = name + "=" : ("; expires=" + expires.toGMTStri
ng())) +
    (expires == null) ? "" : ("; path=" + path)) +
    ((path == null) ? "" : ("; domain=" + domain)) +
    ((domain == null) ? "" : ("; domain=" + domain)) +
    ((secure == true) ? "; secure" : "");
}

function GetCookie(name) {
    var arg = name+"=";
    var alen = arg.length;
    var clen = document.cookie.length;
    var i = 0;
    while (i < clen) {
        var j = i + alen;
        if (document.cookie.substring(i, j) == arg) retu
l(j);
        i = document.cookie.indexOf(" ", i) + 1;
        if (i == 0) break;
    }
    return null;
}

function getCookieVal(offset)
{    var endstr = document.cookie.indexOf (";", offset);
    if (endstr == -1) endstr = document.cookie.length;
    return unescape (document.cookie.substring(offset, endstr));
}

function GetCookie(name) {
    var arg = name+"=";
    var alen = arg.length;
```

COMPUTERS IN THE PAST

The first computers were made by an Englishman named Charles Babbage in 1822. They looked like complicated clocks and worked by wheels and gears. The first electronic computers were made in the 1940s. They were as big as small houses. They often broke down.

One of Babbage's computers is in the Science Museum in London, England.

The first computers used **valves** as big as light bulbs. In the 1950s, **transistors** replaced valves. Computers became smaller and faster. People learned how to make microchips in the 1960s and 1970s. Microchips, or **"chips,"** were small enough for **personal computers** to be made. Today, some computers can fit in your hand.

This is one of the first electronic computers. A modern pocket calculator is more powerful.

BITS AND BYTES

A computer only understands codes. Any information going into a computer must be turned into codes first. The computer uses many tiny electric switches to do this. Each switch equals one **bit** of information. Switches can be ON or OFF. In computer code, ON is "1" and OFF is "0."

This is a magnified picture of a memory chip. Each of the square shapes is a tiny switch. The area shown is about as wide as two human hairs.

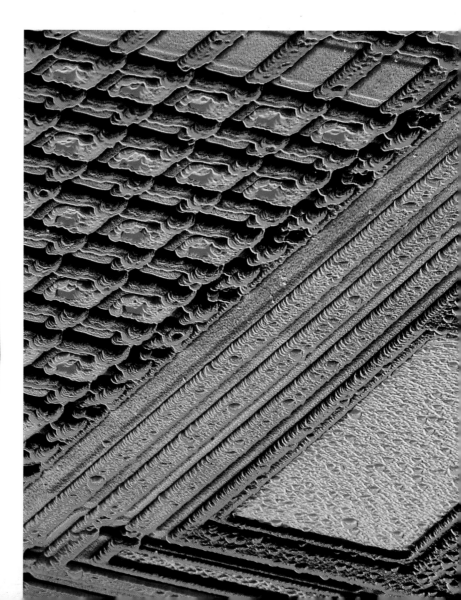

A **program** turns the switches on or off. The number pattern of ONs and OFFs makes a code that the computer understands. Eight switches, or bits, are called a "byte." In computer code, each byte means something. When a key is pressed, the keyboard sends a byte—the code for that key—to the computer.

Each time you play a game on this computer, it will have to process millions of bytes of information.

WHAT IS IN A COMPUTER?

All computers have these four main parts:
- *Inputs* get codes into the system.
- *Processing* arranges codes in a way that the computer can understand.

PROCESSING
- **CPU**
- **memory**
- **sound card**

INPUTS
- **scanner**
- **keyboard**
- **joystick**
- **mouse**

- *Outputs* change codes into words, numbers, pictures, or sounds that people can understand.
- *Storage* saves these words, numbers, pictures, or sounds so that they can be used again.

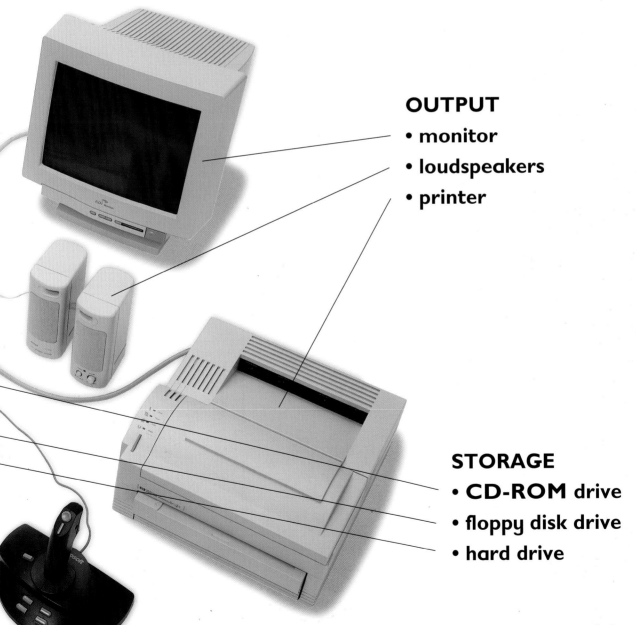

OUTPUT
- **monitor**
- **loudspeakers**
- **printer**

STORAGE
- **CD-ROM** drive
- **floppy disk drive**
- **hard drive**

KEYBOARDS AND MICE

A computer needs the right codes to know what to do. A keyboard has a switch under each key. Most keyboards have more than one hundred switches. When you press keys, the correct codes are sent to the computer. Keyboards are used for writing and for entering **data**.

Pressing a key joins two metal pieces together. This tells the computer which key has been pressed.

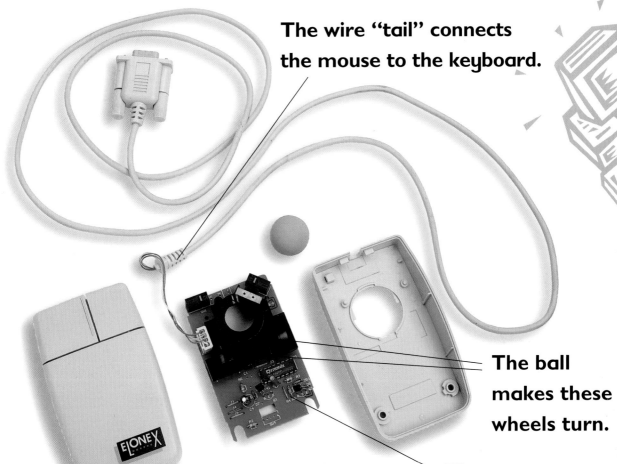

The wire "tail" connects the mouse to the keyboard.

The ball makes these wheels turn.

These switches are turned on when you click a mouse button.

A mouse is an easy way to move the **cursor arrow** around the screen. A mouse can be used to draw shapes or pick items from a list called a menu. When the mouse moves, a ball underneath it rolls, telling the computer how far it has moved. "Clicking" a mouse button sends codes to the computer.

Screens and Printers

You cannot see computer codes. **Monitors** must turn codes into patterns that you can see. Everything on the screen is made of dots called pixels. Each dot can be lit up or dark. A color screen has different colored dots. Sitting back from the screen, you see the picture, not dots.

From close up, you can see the pixels that make the picture.

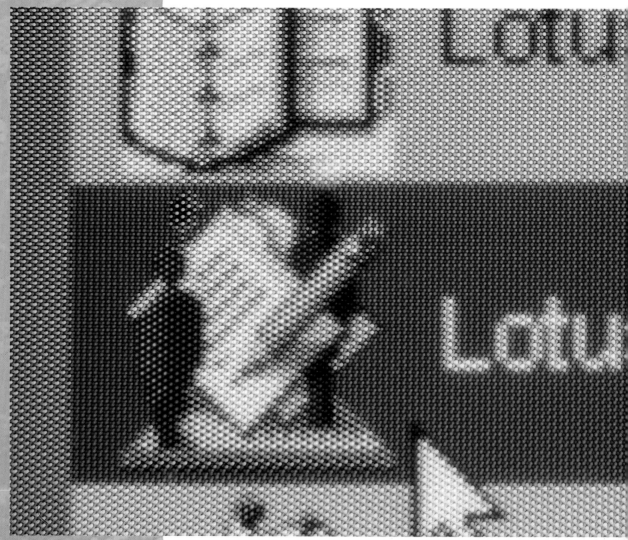

14

A printer makes a picture that you can keep. It turns computer codes into tiny dots of ink on paper. All the words, numbers, and pictures are made of dots joined together. Color printers have four inks—cyan, magenta, yellow, and black. These are mixed together to make thousands of different colors.

This printer squirts ink to make dots on the paper. A full page like this has millions of dots.

15

MEMORY AND PROCESSING

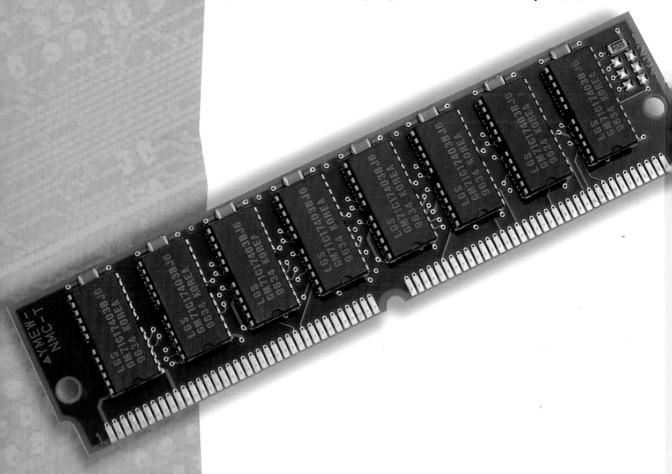

This memory chip plugs into a computer and lets it work faster and run more programs at the same time.

Memory **chips** have millions of switches to store codes. One chip can hold over a million codes. Each million is called a megabyte. This is enough to hold thousands of words. The codes will disappear when the computer is turned off, unless they have been stored in the computer's memory or on a disk.

The processor is the biggest chip in a computer. It does whatever a **program** tells it to do. It takes codes from the memory and changes them. When images on the screen change, the processor has to move the codes for all the pixels to a new place. A processor can change millions of codes every second.

This tiny microprocessor is the "brain" of a computer.

DISKS AND CD-ROMS

Disks hold codes when computers are turned off. They are made of thin plastic. In the plastic are millions of tiny magnets. The magnets are like memory switches, but they do not need electricity. The hard disk, or hard drive, stays in a computer. Floppy disks can be moved.

This brown plastic floppy disk stores codes. The case keeps it from getting dirty.

CD-ROMs hold codes, too. The codes are stored as tiny pits on shiny metal disks. It is hard to change the CD-ROM codes. They are usually used for information that does not need to change. A big encyclopedia can fit on one CD-ROM.

These marks are pits on a **CD-ROM. Five billion can fit on one disk.**

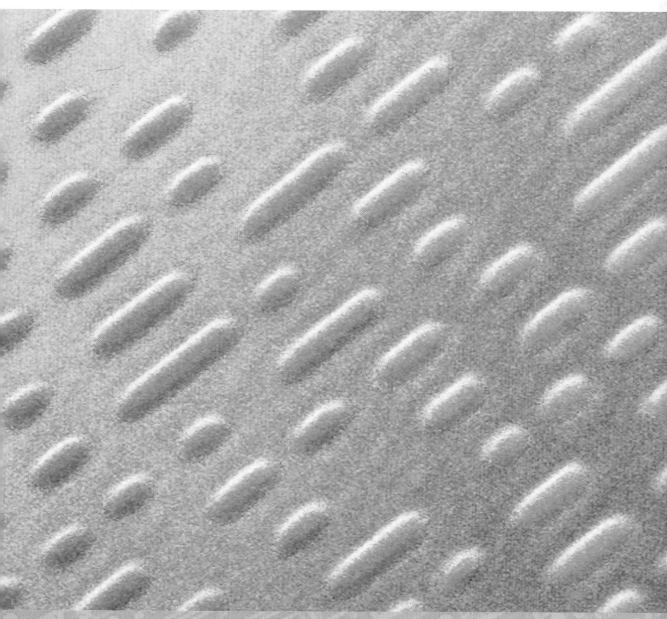

SOFTWARE

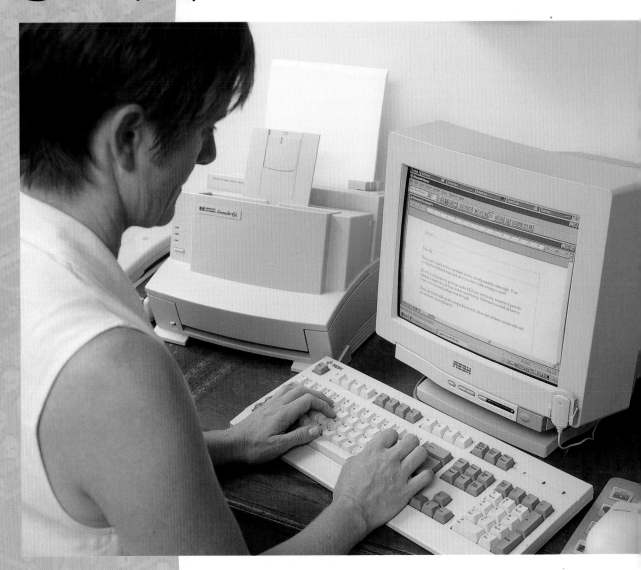

A computer cannot work without an operating system.

Software is another name for **programs**. All computers have an "operating system" program. It starts when the computer is turned on. Windows™ and Mac OS™ are operating systems. All the software used in a computer is controlled by the operating system.

Word processors are software for writing. Other software helps people draw or do math problems. These are called applications. Software is loaded onto a computer hard drive from floppy disks or **CD-ROMs**. It is ready to use whenever you want.

This computer game is a kind of software.

TALKING TO OTHER COMPUTERS

These people work together on a network. They send and share information with each other.

Computers can send codes to each other along wires. Several computers joined like this are called a **network**. Computers in networks share **programs** and extra equipment, like printers. Local networks can cover an entire building. Messages can be sent from one person to someone on another computer in the network.

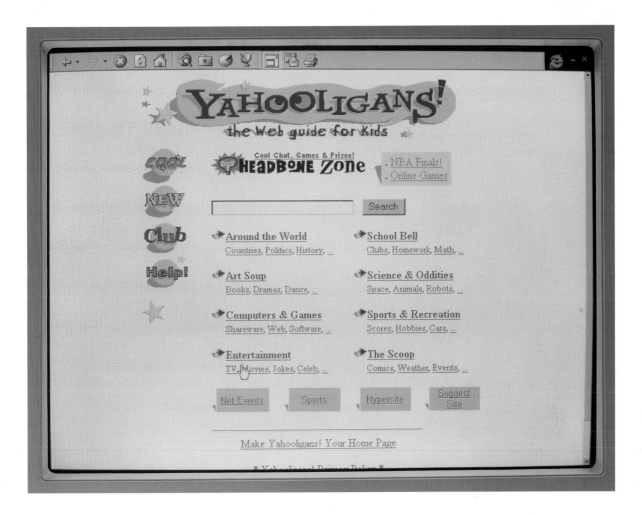

A **modem** turns computer codes into sounds. This lets computers send messages using telephone lines. Modems also turn sound back into codes so that other computers can read the message. Many codes can be sent. They could be writing, numbers, pictures, or sound. A modem lets people send **e-mail**.

The information on this screen has been sent from another computer using a modem and telephone line.

PICTURES AND PIXELS

A scanner has turned the picture into codes. The picture can now be changed.

A scanner turns photos and drawings into codes. Each code stands for the color of one pixel. Each pixel is one dot on the screen. A picture may be made of more than a million pixels. Video cards can turn TV and video pictures into computer codes.

24

Using special software, a computer can change the codes easily. This can be used to change the pictures to create special effects. The colors can be changed. A picture can be stretched or squeezed. Two pictures can be mixed. The pictures can be sent to other computers.

These photographs can be changed and combined on screen using a special program.

SOUND

With a microphone and **sound card**, sounds can be turned into computer codes. The sounds can then be stored in the computer's memory. The sound can be played through loudspeakers. Computers can change the codes to change the sound. Different sounds can be mixed. Special effects like echoes can be added.

Software in this computer turns codes for speech into codes for writing. The computer types on the screen what the user says.

Some software turns human voices into codes. Then, a computer can turn on lights or open doors when a voice tells it to. This helps people who cannot use their hands. Other **programs** turn writing into speech. This helps blind people to read books.

This computer turns written words into codes, then turns the codes into speech sounds.

WHAT'S NEXT?

Computers have changed more than anyone could have imagined. They are getting smaller, faster, and smarter all the time. In your lifetime, new and exciting things are sure to happen. **Virtual reality** may let you explore the universe without leaving your home.

A computer can beat the best human chess players.

Perhaps robots, worked by computers, will do all the things we dislike, like cleaning and washing. One day computers might be able to think for themselves. People may not need to give them **programs** anymore.

Movies and television programs often show robots that are almost like people. One day this might come true!

GLOSSARY

bit   short for "binary digit," which is one switch that is either ON or OFF

CD-ROM   shiny disc that holds words, pictures, and music

chip   (microchip) flat piece of a metal called silicon, containing millions of transistors

cursor arrow flashing arrow on the computer screen that shows where to type or add information

data   information stored in a computer

e-mail   electronic messages sent between computers

memory board   computer part that holds chips and plugs into a computer, adding space to the computer's memory

modem machine that turns computer codes into sounds that can be sent through telephone lines

monitor computer screen

network group of computers that are connected and able to share information and equipment

personal computer (PC) computer that is small enough to sit on a desk

program instructions that tell a computer what to do

sound card computer part that allows a computer to play music and make other sounds

transistor type of electronic switch invented in 1949

valve first type of electronic switch

virtual reality computer-created "world" in which sights and sounds seem real and the user can interact

INDEX

MORE BOOKS TO READ

Holliday, Barbara. *Meet Mr. CPU: An Introduction to the Components of a Personal Computer.* Beverly Hills, Cal: Fun Books, 1997.

Kazunas, Charnan and Thomas Kazunas. *Personal Computers.* Danbury, Conn: Children's Press, 1997.